Come By Here Lord

Everyday Prayers for Children

by Cheryl Willis Hudson
with photographs by Monica Morgan

Come By Here Lord: Everyday Prayers for Children, compiled by Cheryl Willis Hudson
with photographs by Monica Morgan
ISBN: 0-940975-92-0
Copyright © 2001 by Cheryl Willis Hudson
Published by Just Us Books, Inc.
356 Glenwood Avenue
East Orange, NJ 07017
www.justusbooks.com

The copyright holders of individual photographs are listed below:
Front and back cover photographs and photographs on pages 1, 9, 10, 11, 13, 15, 16, 18-19, 20, 21, 22, 24, 25
and 31 copyright © 2001 by Monica Morgan. All rights reserved. Used by permission of the photographer.
page 6, ©Ariel Skelley/The Stock Market
page 29, photograph © 2001 by Norman Bynoe

Acknowledgments
Unless otherwise indicated, all scripture quotations are taken from The Holy Bible, King James Version.
The publishers have made every effort to locate the owners of all copyrighted material and to obtain
permission to reprint the prayers in this book. Any errors are unintentional, and corrections will be made in
future editions if necessary. The publishers gratefully acknowledge the following reproduced herewith:
"A Child's Grace" copyright by Edith Rutter Leatham, William Collins Sons
"Father, We Thank Thee" by Ralph Waldo Emerson
"A Morning Prayer" from An African Prayer Book, copyright 1995 by Desmond Tutu, Doubleday, a division of
Bantam Doubleday Dell Publishing Group, Inc., New York
"Come by Here" (p. 7); "Morning" (p. 8); "Afternoon" (p. 18); "Dear God" (p. 20); "Thank You, Lord" (p. 21)
copyright 2001 by Cheryl Willis Hudson
"I Give Thanks" (p. 25) copyright 2001 by Stephan J. Hudson

We extend very special thanks to members of the Imani Baptist Church of Christ Youth Choir of
East Orange, NJ and their advisor, Florence Claiborne.

Printed in USA   10 9 8 7 6 5 4 3 2 1

Cheryl Willis Hudson is the author of more than one dozen books for children.
Among her published works are AFRO-BETS® ABC Book and AFRO-BETS® 123 Book,
Many Colors of Mother Goose, Hold Christmas in Your Heart, and Bright Eyes, Brown
Skin. Cheryl also edited In Praise of Our Fathers and Our Mothers with her
husband, Wade Hudson. Together, they founded Just Us Books, Inc. Cheryl lives and
works in East Orange, New Jersey.

Monica Morgan is a journalist, public relations specialist, and photographer whose
sensitive portraits have graced the covers and interiors of many international
magazines, newspapers, and corporate publications. She has traveled widely in the
United States, South America, and Africa capturing images of people of African
descent. Come By Here, Lord is Monica's first published book for children. She lives
and works in Detroit, Michigan.

Introduction

In communities across the United States, African-American parents take their children to churches for spiritual nourishment. In their homes, these same parents instruct their children in the values and principles of their faith. Many parents turn to books to help with this instruction and they want at least some of these books to include children who look like their children. But children's books with spiritual themes rarely include children of color. That is why **Come By Here, Lord** was created.

Come By Here, Lord is a collection of simple prayers for children. Some are familiar; others are new. And all are complemented by Bible verses. Parents and children can recite these prayers together any time of the day. And children can also read and recite them alone. These prayers affirm a child's simple faith that God will protect and comfort. They express confidence that God is a source of love. They also declare that God will extend that love wherever we may be.

The words of each prayer in **Come By Here, Lord** are direct and natural, gentle conversations with God. There are prayers that give thanks. Prayers that ask for guidance. Prayers that are simple statements of love for God, family and friends. No matter the subject, these prayers invite children and their parents to stop, chat a while and connect with the Creator. In the African-American tradition, I invite all to "Come By Here."

—Cheryl Willis Hudson

Contents

Introduction   iii

Come By Here   Cheryl Willis Hudson   7

Morning   Cheryl Willis Hudson   8
    God Be in My Head   The Sarum Primer   10
    A Child's Grace   Edith Rutter Leatham   11
    Father, We Thank Thee   Ralph Waldo Emerson   12
    A Morning Prayer   Kenyan Prayer—Boran   14
    The Lord's Prayer   Matthew 6:9-13   17

Afternoon   Cheryl Willis Hudson   18
    Dear God   Cheryl Willis Hudson   20
    Thank You, Lord   Cheryl Willis Hudson   21
    Dear Father, Hear and Bless   Anonymous   22
    I Will Lift Up Mine Eyes   Psalm 121   23

Evening   Anonymous   24
    I Give Thanks   Stephan J. Hudson   25
    The Lord Is My Shepherd   Psalm 23   27
    Make a Joyful Noise   Psalm 100   28
    Bedtime Prayer   Anonymous   30

Epigraph   African Prayer—Traditional   32

Come By Here

Come by here, Lord
Please come by here.
Bless my family, Lord
Keep us free from fear.

Guide our steps, Lord
In work and play.
Come by here, Lord
We ask in prayer today.

But Jesus said, Suffer little children, and forbid
them not to come unto me: for of such is the
kingdom of heaven.   —Matthew 19:14

Morning

I wake up in the morning, Lord
And I give thanks to Thee.
Thank you for the sun and sky.
Thank you for the land and sea.

Thank you for my parents, Lord
And the home that they provide.
Thank you, God, for loving me
And staying by my side.

My voice shalt thou hear in the morning, O Lord; in the morning
will I direct my prayer unto thee, and will look up.

Psalm 5:3

God Be in My Head

God be in my head,
And in my understanding;
God be in my eyes,
And in my looking;
God be in my mouth,
And in my speaking;
God be in my heart,
And in my thinking.

—The Sarum Primer

A Child's Grace

Thank You for the world so sweet,
Thank You for the food we eat,
Thank You for the birds that sing,
Thank You, God, for everything.
—Edith Rutter Leatham

Trust in the Lord with all thine heart; and lean not unto
thine own understanding. In all thy ways acknowledge him,
and he shall direct thy paths.   Proverbs 3:5-6

Father,
We Thank Thee

For flowers that bloom about our feet,
    Father, we thank Thee,
For tender grass so fresh and sweet,
    Father, we thank Thee.
For the song of bird and hum of bee,
For all things fair we hear or see,
Father in heaven, we thank Thee.

For blue of stream and blue of sky,
    Father, we thank Thee,
For pleasant shade of branches high,
    Father, we thank Thee,
For fragrant air and cooling breeze,
For beauty of the blooming trees,
Father in heaven, we thank Thee.

For this new morning with its light,
    Father, we thank Thee,
For rest and shelter of the night,
    Father, we thank Thee,
For health and food, for love and friends,
For everything Thy goodness sends,
Father in heaven, we thank Thee.

                                        —Ralph Waldo Emerson

The earth is the Lord's, and the fullness thereof;
the world, and they that dwell therein.
                        Psalm 24:1

A Morning Prayer

O God, you have let me pass the night
in peace.
Let me pass the day in peace.
Wherever I may go upon my way
which you made peaceable for me,
O God, lead my steps.
When I have spoken, keep lies away
from me.
When I am hungry, keep me
from murmuring.
When I am satisfied, keep me from pride.
Calling upon you, I pass the day,
O Lord, who has no Lord.

— Kenyan Prayer, Boran

Draw nigh to God, and he will draw nigh to you.

James 4:8

The Lord's Prayer

Our Father which art in heaven,
Hallowed be thy name.
Thy kingdom come.Thy will be done in earth,
    as it is in heaven.
Give us this day our daily bread.
And forgive us our debts
    as we forgive our debtors.
And lead us not into temptation,
    but deliver us from evil:
For thine is the kingdom,
    and the power, and the glory, for ever.
Amen.

Matthew 6:9-13

Afternoon

It's afternoon and time to play.

Please keep us safe
and strong.

Protect us
    on the playground, Lord.

            Each and every day.

God is our refuge and strength, a very present
help in trouble.   Psalm 46:1

Dear God

I look up at the clouds, dear God.
They make me think of you.
Clouds dance along the pale blue sky
And Sun plays "peek-a-boo."

Clouds bring the rain that showers grass.
Clouds sprinkle flowers, too.
I dream of floating like a cloud
And I feel close to you.

The heavens declare the glory of God; and the firmament
sheweth his handywork. Psalm 19:1

Thank You, Lord

Thank you, Lord
For this chance for me
    to talk to you.
Thank you for the love
    you give
And all your blessings, too.

Help me to live
    in such a way
That what I do and say
Brings peace and joy
    and kindness
In the world each day.

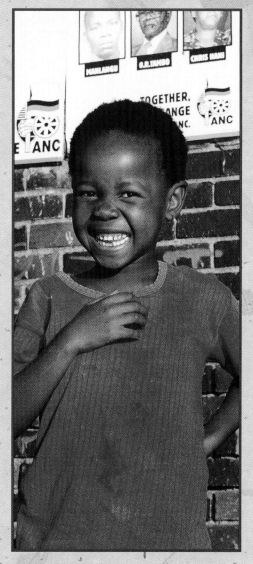

*Blessed are the peacemakers: for they shall be
called the children of God.*   Matthew 5:9

Dear Father, Hear and Bless

Dear Father, hear and bless
   Thy beasts and singing birds:
And guard with tenderness
   Small things that have no words.

—Anonymous

And why take ye thought for raiment? Consider the lilies of the field, how they grow; they toil not, neither do they spin: And yet I say unto you, that even Solomon in all his glory was not arrayed like one of these.

Matthew 6:28-29

I Will Lift Up
Mine Eyes

I will lift up mine eyes unto the hills,
    from whence cometh my help.
My help cometh from the Lord,
    which made heaven and earth.
He will not suffer thy foot to be moved:
He that keepeth thee will not slumber.
Behold, he that keepeth Israel
    shall neither slumber nor sleep.
The Lord is thy keeper:
The Lord is thy shade upon thy right hand.
The sun shall not smite thee by day,
    nor the moon by night.
The Lord shall preserve thee from all evil:
    he shall preserve thy soul.
The Lord shall preserve thy going out
    and thy coming in from this time forth,
    and even for evermore.

Psalm 121

Evening

I hear no voice, I feel no touch
I see no glory bright;
But yet I know that God is near
In darkness as in light.
He watches ever by my side,
And hears my whispered prayer:
The Father for His little child
Both night and day doth care.

—Anonymous

Be still, and know that I am God.

Psalm 46:1

I Give Thanks

Dear Lord,
Thank you for another
    beautiful day.
I give thanks to you
    before in bed I lay.
Please, give me the
    strength tomorrow
    to wake.
But if it is not your will
    to make,
I hope to see you at
    heaven's gate.

And after my soul goes
    high above
Tell Dad and Mom how
    much I've loved.
For they have done
    so much for me
So bless them Lord,
I pray on bended knee.
    —Stephan J. Hudson

Evening, and morning, and at noon, will I
pray, and cry aloud: and he shall hear
my voice.

    Psalm 55:17

The Lord Is My Shepherd

The Lord is my shepherd; I shall not want.
He maketh me to lie down in green pastures:
    he leadeth me beside the still waters.
He restoreth my soul: he leadeth me in the
    paths of righteousness for his name's sake.
Yea, though I walk through the valley of
    the shadow of death, I will fear no evil:
    for thou art with me; thy rod and thy
    staff they comfort me.
Thou preparest a table before me in the
    presence of mine enemies: thou anointest
    my head with oil; my cup runneth over.
Surely goodness and mercy shall follow me
    all the days of my life: and I will dwell in
    the house of the Lord for ever.

Psalm 23

Make a Joyful Noise

Make a joyful noise unto the Lord,
    all ye lands.
Serve the Lord with gladness:
    come before his presence with singing.
Know ye that the Lord he is God:
    it is he that hath made us, and not
    we ourselves; we are his people, and
    the sheep of his pasture.
Enter into his gates with thanksgiving,
    and into his courts with praise:
Be thankful unto him, and bless his name.
For the Lord is good; his mercy
    is everlasting; and his truth endureth
    to all generations.

Psalm 100

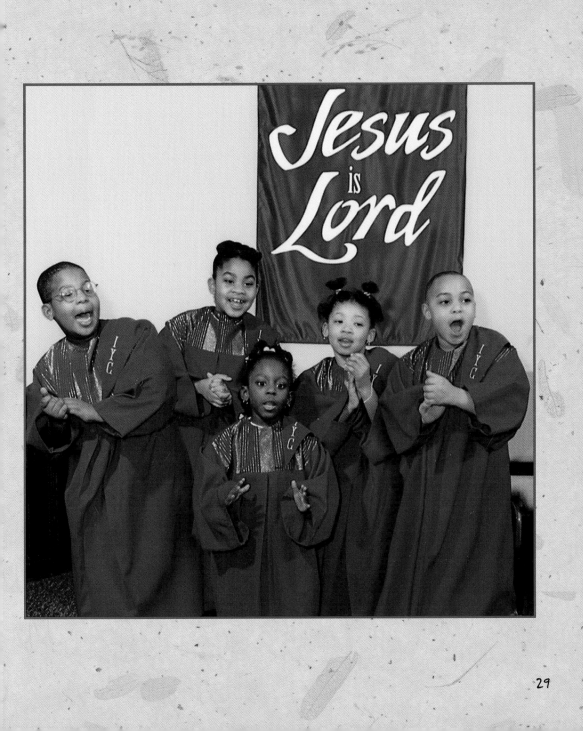

Bedtime Prayer

Now I lay me down to sleep,
I pray Thee, Lord, thy child to keep:
Thy love guard me through the night
And wake me with the morning light.

—Anonymous

I will both lay me down in peace, and sleep: for thou,
Lord, only makest me dwell in safety.   Psalm 4:8

Epigraph

Let us take care of the children,
for they have a long way to go.

Let us take care of the elders,
for they have come a long way.

Let us take care of those in between,
for they are doing the work.
Amen.

—African Prayer
Traditional

The Lord is nigh unto all them that call upon him, to all that call upon
him in truth.   Psalm 145:18